THE RETURN OF
THE BELIEVER

Copyright © 2025 by Jess Condra

All rights reserved. No part of this book may be reproduced, stored in a retrieval system, or transmitted in any form or by any means - electronic, mechanical, photocopying, recording, or otherwise - without the prior written permission of the publisher, except in the case of brief quotations used in reviews or articles.

Published by
Dreamer Publishing

This book is a work of nonfiction. Every effort has been made to ensure accuracy at the time of publication. The author and publisher disclaim any liability from the use or misuse of the information contained herein.

Scripture quotations, unless otherwise noted, are from the Holy Bible, New International Version or respective translation. **Copyright © 1973, 1978, 1984, 2011 by Biblica, Inc.®** Used by permission. All rights reserved worldwide.

Printed in the
United States of America

ISBN: 9798314599082

Table of CONTENTS

Chapter 1: You Are On His Mind 9

Chapter 2: He Still Loves You 13

Chapter 3: Hunted 17

Chapter 4: The Return Of The Believer 21

Chapter 5: Run To The King 25

Chapter 6: Nail It To The Cross 31

Chapter 7: The Prayer Driven Life 37

Chapter 8: It Is What's Inside That Counts 43

Chapter 9: Humility Precedes Honor 49

Chapter 10: Trusting the Architect 57

Chapter 11: Closer 63

Chapter 12: Times Of Refreshing 71

Chapter 13: The Way Back Home 77

Chapter 14: The Courage To Be Who God Created You To Be 81

Chapter 15: It's Time For Your Comeback 87

SECTION 2:
Key Verses For Prayer, Study, and Meditation 91

Dare to Believe

The next morning as they passed by the fig tree he had cursed, the disciples noticed it had withered from the roots up. Peter remembered what Jesus had said to the tree on the previous day and exclaimed, "Look, Rabbi! The fig tree you cursed has withered and died!"

Then Jesus said to the disciples, "Have faith in God. I tell you the truth, you can say to this mountain, 'May you be lifted up and thrown into the sea,' and it will happen. But you must really believe it will happen and have no doubt in your heart. I tell you, you can pray for anything, and if you believe that you've received it, it will be yours. But when you are praying, first forgive anyone you are holding a grudge against, so that your Father in heaven will forgive your sins, too."

MARK 11:20-25 NLT

INTRODUCTION

Return to Me, and I will return to you"

Malachi 3:7

It's time to take back what the enemy has stolen. Satan is now winning on battlegrounds that we once thought were, and would always be, untouchable. His tools of deception have become far too effective among those who call themselves 'believers.' We, the Church, have been empowered by God Himself with the mighty Holy Spirit to carry out His work and purpose, but instead of walking in victory, it seems as if we are losing battles left and right.

That is not God's fault.

Even inside the community of believers, Satan has deceived the hearts and minds of so many, causing them to lose focus and ultimately weakening their faith to the point of spiritual feebleness, creating easy targets for the enemy. This weak level of faith has caused the collapse of entire moral foundations and has spawned an unhealthy disdain for faith on a global scale.

We live in a world that has been conditioned to reject God's truth in favor of personal preference and convenience. Culture has normalized sin, and in many cases, the Church has remained silent. Where we once boldly stood against unrighteousness, many now hesitate, afraid of rejection, ridicule, or the consequences of taking a firm stand for biblical principles. The enemy has capitalized on this spiritual passivity, infiltrating our homes, schools, media, and even our pulpits with diluted doctrine and half-truths that leave believers spiritually malnourished and unprepared for battle.

But there is hope.

God has not abandoned His people. His call is still clear:

>
>
> *Return to Me, and I will return to you"*
>
> **Malachi 3:7**

The power of true believers is not found in political policies, cultural trends, or human philosophies, it is found in absolute consecration to God. When we surrender fully to Him, aligning our lives with His will, we will see the tides turn. We will witness revival, not just in our churches but in our homes, communities, and nations.

It is our responsibility to remove sin and compromise as accepted norms in society. We owe it to our ancestors who lived before us, our children, ourselves, and most of all, to God. We must reach for the standard that God expects of us and be the Salt and Light of this world. Legislation can't do it, and positive thinking alone isn't enough. The solution to the brokenness we see around us is not found in worldly wisdom but in a return to genuine faith.

We must awaken. We must rise up in the mighty name of Jesus. We must reclaim what was lost.

Consecration to God is the only way.

CHAPTER 1

YOU ARE ON HIS MIND

Take comfort in the fact that God knows precisely where you are at this very moment and is fully aware of the journey that led you here. When He examines our circumstances, fear and anxiety hold no place in His divine heart. He is the Almighty, the Master Potter who created and continues to shape us, the Great Physician who heals us, and the Architect of the Ages who designed and created everything inside and outside of this universe. In this very moment, although it might not seem possible, He is masterfully orchestrating your life for a triumphant comeback.

God is well aware of the level of pressure you can withstand and is actively monitoring your situation very closely. We may not understand everything about our current set of circumstances, and we certainly don't have all the answers, but He does. Our problems are not a mystery to the King of all Kings. God is not losing sleep over the economy, our children, our issues at work, or the price of a gallon of gasoline. He isn't worried about it one iota. Heaven is not going through a recession or experiencing any shortages, and God is still on His throne.

We must realize that God, our heavenly Father, knows the beginning from the end. His infinite wisdom allowed prophecies to be foretold hundreds if not thousands of years before they were fulfilled. He knew you before you were even formed in your mother's womb, and His word says that even the hairs of your head are numbered. Know with certainty that God hasn't forgotten about you. He genuinely cares for you, and His purpose for your life involves becoming a bright beacon of faith and hope, shining His light to all those you encounter.

He sees your struggles, your victories, and even the moments when you feel unseen. Nothing escapes His attention, and no burden you carry is too small for Him to care about. His love for you is unwavering, and His plans are greater than anything you could imagine. Though life may bring uncertainty, trials, and unexpected detours, God remains steadfast, guiding your steps with a purpose that is beyond human understanding.

Trust that He is working behind the scenes, aligning every situation for your good. When doubts creep in, remember that He has never abandoned His people, and He won't start now. His promises are true, His timing is perfect, and His grace is more than enough. Stay rooted in His word, walk in faith, and know that you are never alone. He is always with you, leading you into a future filled with hope and divine purpose.

He wants you to know that you are on His mind.

HEART CHECK

Take a deep breath and let this truth settle in: you are on His mind. The God who created the universe is not distant or indifferent; He is intimately aware of your life, your struggles, and your victories.

- ✞ Do you truly believe that God is orchestrating your life, even when things feel uncertain?
- ✞ What worries or anxieties have been taking up space in your heart that you need to release to Him today?
- ✞ How does knowing that He knows every detail about you change the way you see your current situation?

Pray and Believe:

Whisper a prayer of surrender, thanking Him for His faithfulness. Let His peace replace your fear, and rest in the assurance that He has not forgotten you.

CHAPTER 2

HE STILL LOVES YOU

Thousands of churches in America are closing their doors every year. What's even more alarming is that approximately only 45 percent of Americans identify as followers of Christ, and only 20 percent attend a church service at least once a week. To put this in perspective, more than 50 years ago, that number was as high as 70 to 80 percent in certain areas of the country.

The Bible foretold this long ago by saying

There would be a time in the last days when, among other things, people would become lovers of pleasure more than they are lovers of God."

2 Timothy 3:1

How significant is this decline?

While many scoff at those statistics as though they were mere burger joints going out of business, the true effect is nothing short of tragic. It has been detrimental to our nation. On a macro level, this trend represents the moral collapse of our culture. On a micro level, it represents family members or friends who have chosen to walk away from their faith, only to find the path they chose to follow was in the opposite direction of God's will for their lives.

When King Jesus told us the story of the Prodigal Son **(See Luke 15:11-32),** he did so knowing that it would have a profound effect on all who heard its message. He knew we would all be able to relate in one way or another. King Jesus was illustrating that regardless of what path we choose, God knows where we are. He understands our needs, and our Heavenly Father will always be eager to welcome us home.

Understand this: there is no path you can take that escapes the knowledge, wisdom, or reach of God. We can't go so far that we outrun him or are hidden from him. He notices every decision we make. He sees the paths we choose, and he is keenly aware of the intentions of our hearts. Regardless of who you are, where you've been, or what you've done, he knows where you are. He sees you in your current circumstances, and he is the only one who has true answers.

The Bible puts it this way,

And I am convinced that nothing can ever separate us from God's love. Neither death nor life. Neither angels nor demons. Neither our fears for today nor our worries about tomorrow. Not even the powers of hell can separate us from God's love. No power in the sky above or in the earth below. Indeed nothing in all creation will ever be able to separate us from the love of God that is revealed in Christ Jesus our Lord.'
Romans 8:38-39

Simply put, He still cares about you. He still loves you.

HEART CHECK

No matter how far you feel from God, His love for you has never wavered. He has seen every struggle, every wrong turn, and every moment of doubt. But, his arms remain open, ready to welcome you home.

- ✝ Have you ever felt like you've drifted too far from God's love? What does Romans 8:38-39 say about that?
- ✝ Are there areas of your life where you've believed the lie that God is distant or uninterested in you?
- ✝ What would it look like for you to take a step back toward Him today?

Pray and Believe:

Let go of any shame or hesitation. Whisper this simple prayer:

"Father, I know You still love me. Help me to rest in that truth and draw near to You again."

CHAPTER 3
HUNTED

Our spiritual enemy, relentless and cunning, wages war against us on all fronts. He is well-versed in our vulnerabilities, carefully studying them to capitalize on our weaknesses. Like a patient sniper, he waits for the opportune moment to strike, seeking to undermine our faith and steer us away from God's path. If he cannot make progress with us directly, he turns to those closest to us, our friends and relatives, in an attempt to gain access to our weaknesses or areas of susceptibility.

Throughout the course of our lives, we may witness individuals within our circle who once embraced the faith slowly drift away. They have been hunted, one by one, falling prey to the enemy's insidious suggestions, lies, and schemes. The enemy operates with precise calculation, strategically targeting each person. His temptations and tactics span a wide spectrum, custom-tailored for each individual's unique vulnerabilities.

What may work on one person may not work on another. In some instances, where you find strength, your spouse may struggle, or perhaps you have triumphed over a particular test, but your children find themselves struggling with similar challenges. Satan, in his relentless pursuit, will employ whatever means necessary to keep you defeated. That is his mission.

In **John 10:10**, we are reminded that the enemy's purpose is nothing short of destroying us. But in stark contrast, Jesus has come so that we may have life and have it abundantly. When we gather the courage to take a step, or even a giant leap, of faith we should not be surprised if the enemy comes knocking on our door, desperately trying to keep us in check.

It almost sounds like a plotline straight out of a science fiction film, in which we find ourselves cast as the central characters in an epic struggle. However, the truth is that this narrative is all too real. The battle between light and darkness, good and evil, has been waged since the beginning of time, and we are called to actively engage in this spiritual warfare.

We must equip ourselves with the armor of God, as described in **Ephesians 6:10-18.** By hearing the Word of God, praying, fasting, and studying the Scriptures, we fortify our spiritual defenses, enabling us to stand firm against the enemy's attacks.

Moreover, we should not walk this path alone, for God has blessed us with a community of believers who can provide support, encouragement, and accountability.

We must remain vigilant, recognizing that the enemy is always seeking opportunities to exploit our weaknesses. When confronted with temptations and trials, we can turn to Jesus, our ultimate source of strength and victory. He has overcome the world, and in him we find the power to resist the schemes of the evil one.

Though the battle may be fierce, we can rest assured that victory is assured as we walk with Christ.

HEART CHECK

The enemy may be relentless, but God's power within you is greater. You are not defenseless, and you are not alone in this battle.

- ✞ Where have you noticed spiritual attacks in your life or the lives of those around you?
- ✞ Have you been proactive in putting on the armor of God, or have you been leaving yourself vulnerable?
- ✞ What steps can you take today to strengthen your spiritual defenses through prayer, scripture, and community?

Pray and Believe: Ask God to open your eyes to the enemy's tactics and to strengthen you for the battle. Pray:

"Lord, I know the enemy is hunting, but I trust that You are my protector. Help me stand firm in Your strength and not my own."

Remember that you are not just being hunted, you are also being defended by the Almighty. Walk in that confidence.

CHAPTER 4

THE RETURN OF THE BELIEVER

The heaviness of the situation in which you currently find yourself is nothing more than a grain of sand in the hand of our Heavenly Father. How far away you've traveled from the path of His will for your life has not created an obstacle too great for Him to overcome. I know from personal experience, it's easy to get yourself involved in some real doozies, but God always knows just how to take care of us.

There have been moments (probably more than I care to share) when I have had the perfect setup but still managed to make a mess of things. The skies were blue, the temperature was cool, the birds were singing, and the fairway was beautiful. And although the ball was teed up for me just right, I still found a way to hook it directly into the bunker. The conditions couldn't have been better, but somehow I still found a way to do exactly what I wasn't supposed to.

Have you ever felt that way?

Far too often, those who begin their journey on the right road find themselves in the ditch, or even worse, following a road that's in the opposite direction of what our Heavenly Father has planned out for them. (Ask Mr. Jonah.) God wants us to walk with Him and not get distracted by anything that is trying to pull our attention away. It's true, the God who created heaven and earth wants you to walk with Him. He wants to enjoy time together, laugh together, and even go through dark and dangerous places together. That's why King David wrote that although he walked through the valley of the shadow of death, he wouldn't fear evil or anything that would come against him. **(See Psalm 23)** He didn't fear because he said, as a good shepherd, God's rod and staff were always there to protect him from danger. King David found confidence and safety in walking with God because he realized that God's weapons were far more powerful than any enemy that may come his way.

Contrary to popular belief, God is not a schoolyard bully just waiting for any chance He can get to whack you with His baseball bat. That's not who He is at all. Your image of our Heavenly Father matters. If you see Him as someone you should run from, you are seeing Him all wrong. God has your best interest at heart. He wants you to trust Him. And you should trust Him. You should trust Him enough to know that the path He has laid out for your life is the very best possible path you could take.

But what happens when we opt in on our own way? What happens when we say to God, "No thanks, I've got this"? God, as a gentleman, will kindly accommodate your request. B esides, love is not possible without free will. Although He has been known to be very persuasive at times, He wants you to make the quality decision to choose the path He has prepared for you.

In the parable of the prodigal son **(See Luke 15)** God displays how He truly views us even when we are demanding and disobedient. He isn't waiting to punish us. That isn't something that He receives joy from. Our Heavenly Father is waiting for us to make the quality decision to travel back in the direction of home, where He can lavish us with love that only He can give.

Where do you find yourself at this very moment? Are you basking in the warmth of God's love and grace, or do you find yourself running away from the life that God has prepared for you? My friend, you know the answer to this question. It's a question that has only two answers. This isn't one of those questions that you can charm your way out of. The answer to this question requires a direct "yes" or "no." God doesn't accept "kind of" or "I intend to get around to it." He either wants you to be on fire for Him, or ice cold. He doesn't accept lukewarmness (See **Revelation 3:16 NLT,** or if you are feeling particularly brave, read that verse in the Message Translation).

His desire for you is to live in a way that brings Him glory and advances the Kingdom that Jesus created for us. So, regardless of where you find yourself at this very moment, even if you are dining with swine, God still wants you back. There is still room for you at the table, He has reserved it just for you. Your name is there, it's your seat, and he wants you to be in your rightful place as his son or daughter.

It's time to return to your Father's house.

HEART CHECK

No matter how far you've strayed, God is still calling you home. His love has not diminished, and His plans for you remain. The only question is: will you turn back to Him?

- ✝ Are you walking in step with God, or have you taken a detour from His path for your life?
- ✝ What fears, doubts, or excuses have kept you from fully surrendering to Him?
- ✝ If you knew God was running toward you with open arms, how would that change your response to Him today?

Pray and Believe: If your heart has wandered, don't waste another moment. Say this simple but powerful prayer:

"Father, I'm coming home. I know You've been waiting; I now surrender my life to you."

Your seat at His table is still waiting. Now is the time to take your place.

CHAPTER 5

RUN TO THE KING

The world we live in is full of deception. It's found in every corner of our life because it has been woven deeply into the fabric of our culture and societies by the evil one. It can be found in business meetings, contracts, casual conversations, commercials, fashion, consumer products, favors, music, movies, and much more.

Deception is everywhere. Jesus even warned there was deceitfulness in riches **(See Matthew 13:22)**, and the Apostle Paul admonished us to not be deceived in that whatever a person sows, they will also reap. **(See Galations 6:7)** Although we may not want to admit that it can happen, we can easily be deceived by others, by temptations, and we can even deceive ourselves.

The reason I say this is because you need to know that if you've fallen prey to sin or deception you are certainly not alone, and you must not allow the enemy to use bad decisions you've made to make you feel inferior, unworthy, disqualified, or feel that you are in a hopeless situation. We have all made bad decisions. We have all been guilty of sin. **(See Romans 3:23)** However, we also all have the opportunity to be free from whatever bondage we have been trapped in. The bible says,

If we confess our sins, He is faithful and just to forgive us our sins and to cleanse us from all unrighteousness."

1 John 1:9

That is true hope. This means that even if we find ourselves dining with the pigs, our heavenly Father still holds a seat for us at His house, where we truly belong. **(See Luke 15:16)**

In the Kingdom of God, Jesus is King. He is Lord of all, and has been given all power, wisdom, and dominion over all of creation. There is no name that can stand next to the mighty name of Jesus, and there is no other name given to humanity by which we can be saved from sin and inherit eternal life. **(See Acts 4:12)** If you find yourself in a situation where you have been hunted by the enemy as vulnerable prey, and even if you are a long way from home, I have one message for you: run to the King. Run to the King and never look back.

Completely leave the situation you are in, and run to Him. He has all of the answers. Proverbs tells us that *'when the King smiles there is life, and his favor refreshes like a spring rain.'* **(See Proverbs 16:15 NLT)** You just need to find the courage to leave where you are and run to him.

- ✞ Don't allow pride to keep you where you are. Run to the King.
- ✞ Don't allow the lure and deception of sin keep you in bondage. Run to the King.
- ✞ Don't allow past mistakes to prevent you from reaching your Godly destiny. Run to the King.
- ✞ Don't allow the lying voice of the enemy, even if it's being shouted by someone you love, keep you in defeat. Run to the King.
- ✞ Don't allow potential embarrassment to keep you in your current situation. Run to the King.

Hear the powerful words the Lord Himself spoke to Joshua after Moses died:

>
>
> *Arise.' 'No man shall be able to stand before you.' 'Every place your foot touches, I will give to you.' 'As I was with Moses, so I will be with you.' 'I will not leave you nor forsake you.' 'Be strong and of good courage.' 'Do not be afraid, for I will be with you wherever you go.'*
>
> **Joshua Chapter 1**

If you look close enough you'll find the enemy working over-time to prevent us from leaving dark circumstances because you are exactly where he wants you to be. He will lie, deceive, keep you in check, hinder, and use anything he can to keep you where you are. Don't listen to his voice! There is only one voice that you should listen to, and it is the voice of the one who truly loves you. It is the voice of the one who gave himself for you, and loves you unconditionally. If you will allow yourself to be still and quiet you can hear His voice. He is saying 'return to me.' He is saying 'I love you.' He is reassuring you there is still hope. Regardless of where you've been or how far you have wandered, He wants you to know that you haven't gone too far.

What is it about people that makes them want to hold on to what they have, even if what they have is the very thing that is holding them back or even destroying them? What is it about us that makes us not want to let go? It is, very simply, a lack of faith and/or fear of the future. When Jesus and His disciples were crossing the Sea of Galilee, He woke up and calmed the storm. He then immediately turned to His disciples and asked, 'Where is your faith?' (See Luke 8:25) He didn't ask them if they had any faith, He asked them where it was. Their faith was simply misplaced.

It's easy to look at the disciples and point a judgemental finger, after all they were with Jesus. Why did they have anything to be afraid of? Can I tell you, we are in the same boat. When the storms of life are thundering all around us do we go directly to Jesus, or do we sulk back in fear? Do we see the lightning bolts and the high waves and think, 'well this is it, it's over for me?' Jesus is still asking the same question and this time it is directed at us, 'Where is your faith?' Your faith is somewhere, and it is in something or someone. It may be in your own strength, your wealth, your knowledge, or even in your fear; but, your faith is somewhere. And, whether you realize it or not, you are exercising your faith right at this very moment. The key is to place your faith in the one who has your best interest at heart, the one who truly loves you. Regardless of the storm you are in, the answer is the same; we must place our faith in King Jesus. He has the answers for your situation, and if you listen closely, you can hear Him calling, 'Come back to me.'

Run to the King and never look back.

HEART CHECK

The enemy will use every tactic to keep you where you are; fear, pride, deception, and even shame. But there is only one right response when you realize you need to return to God: Run to the King.

- ✞ What is holding you back from running fully to Jesus? Is it fear? Doubt? Pride?
- ✞ Are you listening to the enemy's lies, or are you tuning in to the voice of the One who truly loves you?
- ✞ Where is your faith right now? Is it placed in your circumstances, your own strength, or in Christ alone?

Pray and Believe: Take a deep breath and surrender your hesitation. Say this prayer:

"Lord, I hear Your voice calling me back. I refuse to stay in this place any longer. I run to You with my whole heart."

No more looking back. No more hesitation. The King is waiting. Run to Him.

CHAPTER 6
NAIL IT TO THE CROSS

In a world full of distractions, the ramifications and implications of sin have been almost completely suppressed. However, God doesn't look at it that way. God is still serious about sin, and the Bible tells us that all unrighteousness is sin. **(See 1 John 5:17)** Sin is anything that is contrary to the will of God. Simply put, it is any thought, action, or attitude that deviates from God's standard.

Understand this: God loves you unconditionally, but he does not have unconditional tolerance for sin in your life.

As a child I would frequently hear preachers recite the list of the 'works of the flesh' that the Apostle Paul listed in Galations the fifth chapter: 'When you follow the desires of your sinful nature, the results are very clear: sexual immorality, impurity, lustful pleasures, idolatry, sorcery, hostility, quarreling, jealousy, outbursts of anger, selfish ambition, dissension, division, envy, drunkenness, wild parties, and other sins like these. Let me tell you again, as I have before, that anyone living that sort of life will not inherit the Kingdom of God.' **(See Galations 5:19-21)**

However, even that is not a conclusive list. He also wrote in the first chapter of the book of Romans, 'Their lives became full of every kind of wickedness, sin, greed, hate, envy, murder, quarreling, deception, malicious behavior, and gossip. They are backstabbers, haters of God, insolent, proud, and boastful. They invent new ways of sinning, and they disobey their parents. They refuse to understand, break their promises, are heartless, and have no mercy. They know God's justice requires that those who do these things deserve to die, yet they do them anyway. Worse yet, they encourage others to do them, too.' **(See Romans 1:29-32)** This passage thoroughly describes the depth of human sinfulness when people reject God, leading to a corrupt and unrighteous lifestyle.

As a child I had no idea of the importance of those scriptures. Now, after a few years behind me and, most importantly, after growing closer to God and learning more about Him, I have increasingly come to realize the importance of following teachings on avoiding sin and living a Godly life. The bible tells us that the penalty for sin is, and always has been, death. Eternal death, which is, besides hot flames, existing apart from God forever. And, not only are there eternal consequences to sin, there are severe consequences for our natural, non-eternal, lives here and now as well.

Here's the good news: Jesus paid our sin debt for us in its entirety. If we turn from our sinfulness and put our trust in him, He promises to remove the guilt of sin from our lives completely. When God looks upon the heart of the believer he no longer sees his or her sin, He sees the blood of Jesus applied to a believing heart. He sees us just as righteous as Jesus is. Think about that for a moment! I love how the great prophet Isaiah said it,

Though your sins be as scarlet, they Shall be white as snow; Though they are red like crimson, They shall be as wool."
Isaiah 1:18

Living a life of sin is beneath the child of God. You have been called to live separate from this world. The old way of living according to your own sinful and fleshly desires are now a thing of the past, and are never to be revisited again. You now have a mandate; a job to do for God. Your mandate is to represent the Lord, His Kingdom, and His family by living a life of Godly excellence according to His word. God's desire for you is to be an example of what it looks like to reject what the world is offering, and fully embrace Godly living. Your heavenly Father is perfectly Holy, and His desire for you is to live Holy as well.

When you adopt a 'Kingdom of God' way of living your life will produce Godly Fruit: 'But the Holy Spirit produces this kind of fruit in our lives: love, joy, peace, patience, kindness, goodness, faithfulness, gentleness, and self-control. There is no law against these things!' **(See Galations 5:22-23)** I love how the Bible tells us there is no law against these things. That means you can be as good as you want to be, without limit!

Do you see the stark difference in these two different lifestyles? And, yes they are lifestyles. One person is a slave to this world culture and their own desires, and the other is a servant of the Lord Jesus. One lifestyle lives to please themselves, and the other lives to please God. One walks among darkness, and the other basks in God's glorious light. One constantly produces sin, while the Godly person is a tree of life that consistently produces good fruit.

So, how do we follow the Lord Jesus the way he wants us to? He said it simply,

If any of you wants to be my follower, you must give up your own way, take up your cross daily, and follow me.' (See Luke 9:23) We must crucify our own flesh, and die to the sinful nature we were born with. 'Those who belong to Christ Jesus have nailed the passions and desires of their sinful nature to his cross and crucified them there."

Galations 5:24

People often say something to the effect of, 'It's impossible to live that way; I simply can't live everyday without doing the things I always have.' Well, they would be correct. It is impossible to live a Holy life, naturally speaking. But, what they are not factoring into the equation is that when Jesus returned to the Father, he didn't leave us hanging. He didn't just say, 'Goodbye, I hope y'all do good.' No, far from it. He said that when he went away he would send us a helper. And He did. Our helper is the Holy Spirit.

God's Holy Spirit guides us, comforts us, teaches us, admonishes us, convicts us, and is with us with the distinct purpose of assisting us in being able to follow-through with God's will for our lives. He, the Holy Spirit, gives us the power to overcome sin in any situation we may find ourselves in. The Bible tells us,

>
> *The temptations in your life are no different from what others experience. And God is faithful. He will not allow the temptation to be more than you can stand. When you are tempted, he will show you a way out so that you can endure."*
> **1 Corinthians 10:13 NLT**

The main idea for us to consider is that we must nail our sin to the cross. This effectively means to kill the sin that lives within us. This is, in part, what Jesus meant when he said, 'If you try to hang on to your life, you will lose it. But if you give up your life for my sake, you will save it.' **(See Matthew 16:25)** There is no room for debate on this.

Jesus demands and deserves absolute obedience. Not partial obedience. Not delayed obedience. He expects absolute obedience. He is King, and we are servants in His Kingdom. **(See John 14:15)**

HEART CHECK

The call to follow Jesus is not a casual invitation, it's a call to surrender. He asks us to nail our sin to the cross, to leave behind our old way of living, and to walk in the new life He has given us.

- ✝ What sins or struggles are you still holding onto that need to be nailed to the cross?
- ✝ Are you living in full obedience to Jesus, or are there areas where you've been hesitant to fully surrender?
- ✝ How can you rely on the Holy Spirit more in your daily life to overcome temptation and walk in holiness?

Pray and Believe: Ask the Holy Spirit to reveal anything in your life that needs to be surrendered to Jesus. Pray:

"Lord, I don't want to carry this sin any longer. I surrender it to You. Help me to walk in the power of Your Spirit and live a life that brings You glory."

The cross is not just a symbol, it's the place where sin is put to death. Nail it there, and never take it back.

CHAPTER 7

THE PRAYER DRIVEN LIFE

Have you ever noticed how prayer ist treated like a last resort? Like those 'break glass in case of emergency' signs? We wait until life is falling apart, and then suddenly we remember that we should probably pray about it. But what if prayer wasn't just a backup plan? What if it was the plan?

What if we lived a prayer-driven life?

A prayer-driven life isn't just about saying a quick blessing over your food or tossing up a request when you are in a tough spot. It is about living in constant conversation with God, walking, talking, listening, and depending on Him every single day, in every situation. Prayer is not just something you do. It is a major part of your life everyday. The apostle Paul wrote that we should, *"Pray without ceasing."* **(See 1 Thessalonians 5:14)**

Think about this. Jesus, the Son of God, needed to pray. Over and over in Scripture, we see Him stepping away to talk to the Father. **Luke 5:16** says, *"Jesus often withdrew himself and prayed."* If the Savior of the world needed time with God, how much more do we?

Prayer is not just about getting answers. It is about cultivating a relationship with our heavenly Father. God never intended prayer to be some religious task we check off. He wants a real, ongoing conversation with us. Just like you would talk to a close friend, that is how prayer should feel; natural, honest, and constant.

Something truly powerful happens when we pray. It is not just about asking God to fix our problems or change our circumstances, though He certainly does that. It is about how prayer transforms us from the inside out.

When we commit to a life of prayer, we begin to see everything differently. Our hearts, once weighed down by worry, start to rest in God's peace. Our attitudes, once shaped by frustration or fear, begin to reflect faith and hope.

Our perspectives, once focused on what we can see and control, shift to a bigger picture, one that reveals God's plan, His timing, and His goodness.

A life built on prayer is a life built on peace because when we talk to God consistently, we are reminded that He is in control and we do not have to carry the weight of the world on our shoulders. It is a life built on wisdom because the more we seek Him, the more He reveals His ways, giving us clarity in decisions both big and small. It is a life built on divine direction because when we pray, we invite God to lead us instead of trying to figure everything out on our own. We learn to trust that even when the path ahead is unclear, God is faithfully leading us forward, one step at a time.

Prayer does not just change what happens around us. It changes who we are. It shapes us into people who reflect Christ in the way we think, speak, and live. It is not just about what we ask for. It is about who we become in the process.

The alternative is living on our own strength, making decisions based on feelings, reacting instead of seeking. A prayer-driven life is different because it surrenders control to God. It says, *"Lord, I trust You more than I trust myself."* And let's be real. He is much better at running our lives than we are.

Honestly, prayer can be hard. Distractions, doubt, and discouragement all get in the way. Have you ever sat down to pray and suddenly remembered everything you forgot to put on your grocery list? Or started praying only to find yourself checking your phone three minutes later?

The enemy would love nothing more than to keep you too busy, too tired, or too discouraged to pray. Why? Because he knows prayer is powerful.

So how do we push through? We make prayer a priority. We carve out time just like we do for everything else that matters. We remind ourselves that prayer is not about being perfect. It is about being present with God.

Think about Daniel. He prayed three times a day, even when it could have cost him his life. Or, how about pastor Jim Cymbala of the Brooklyn Tabernacle who has built his entire ministry on the power of prayer. When he took over the struggling church in New York City, it had barely a handful of members, no money, and no clear direction. But instead of relying on strategies or programs, he committed to prayer. Week after week, he and his congregation sought God, asking for His presence to fill their church and transform lives, and God answered in incredible ways.

The Brooklyn Tabernacle grew not just in numbers, but in testimonies of radical life change. Addicts were set free, broken families were restored, and people far from God found salvation. Cymbala often said that prayer was the engine that moved everything in his ministry, not just a part of it. These were not special people with some elite access to God. They just believed in the power of prayer and lived like it mattered.

A prayer-driven life means prayer is not just something you do. It is how you move through the world. You pray before big decisions, but you also pray in the small moments. You pray when you are happy, when you are frustrated, and when you are unsure. You talk to God like He is right there, because He is.

Want to make prayer a bigger part of your life? Start simple. Set a time. It does not have to be an hour-long session. Start with five minutes. Pray Scripture. God's Word is full of powerful prayers you can use. Be honest. God is not impressed with fancy words, He wants your heart.

Listening in prayer is just as, or more important than, talking. It is about hearing from Him. Write it down. Keep a prayer journal and watch how God moves over time. The goal is not to follow a formula. It is to build a habit of staying connected to God.

I remember when our youngest son was returning home from the Marine Corps. He had fallen into a dangerous set of ungodly habits, and honestly, was struggling to find his way. One night while my wife was speaking with him on the phone she gave the wisest and simplest direction. She simply said, *"Son, just talk to God."* Don't worry about church. Don't worry about your habits right now. Don't worry about religion. Just talk to God. That advice was the beginning of the restoration of his walk with Jesus. He was far from home, but his direction changed. God heard him. God listened. God helped him.

The more you pray, the more you will notice something incredible. Peace. Strength. Clarity. Confidence. When prayer is your first response instead of your last resort, your faith grows. You start seeing God at work in the little things. And here is the best part. When your life is fueled by prayer, you inspire others to do the same. You become a walking testimony of what it looks like to live in step with God.

We must stop treating prayer like a spare tire and start making it the steering wheel. Build your life where talking to God is not just a habit. It is the heartbeat of everything you do.

Make the quality commitment today to live a prayer-driven life.

HEART CHECK

Prayer is not just something we do, it's the foundation of a life fully surrendered to God. It's not a last resort; it's the steering wheel that directs everything we do.

- ✝ How often do you rely on prayer as your first response rather than your backup plan?
- ✝ Are you prioritizing time with God, or is prayer getting crowded out by distractions?
- ✝ What would change in your life if you truly lived a prayer-driven life?

Pray and Believe: Right now, before you move on, take a moment to pray. It doesn't have to be long or polished. Just talk to God. Say:

"Lord, I don't want to treat prayer as an afterthought. Teach me to walk with You daily, to seek You first, and to trust that You are listening. Let my life be prayer-driven, not driven by fear, problems, and anxiety."

Your next step is simple, just talk to God. Make prayer the priority, not the backup plan.

CHAPTER 8

IT IS WHAT'S INSIDE THAT COUNTS

We live in a world that teaches us to focus on the outside. People care about appearances, reputation, and checking the right boxes. But God isn't fooled by any of it. He sees deeper, past our words, past our actions, all the way into our hearts.

Hebrews 4:12 says, *"For the word of God is living and active, sharper than any two-edged sword, piercing to the division of soul and spirit, of joints and marrow, and discerning the thoughts and intentions of the heart."* That means God doesn't just see what we do. He knows why we do it. He knows what we think before we ever act. That's why real righteousness isn't about trying harder to be good. It's about actually being transformed from the inside out.

Jesus made this clear in the Sermon on the Mount when He openly raised the standard of righteousness. The religious leaders of His day focused on following the law externally, but Jesus exposed a deeper truth. Sin doesn't start with an action, it starts with a thought. He said,

> ❝
>
> *You have heard that it was said, 'You shall not commit adultery.' But I say to you that everyone who looks at a woman with lustful intent has already committed adultery with her in his heart"*
>
> **Matthew 5:27-28**

That's a sobering thought. According to Jesus, it's not enough to avoid sinful actions. We must guard against sinful thoughts. The battle is won or lost in the mind.

Think about a married man at the gym. He doesn't flirt, doesn't approach anyone, and would never cheat on his wife. But when an attractive woman walks by, he allows his thoughts to linger. He excuses it by saying he isn't acting on it. But Jesus says otherwise. Sin isn't just about behavior. It's about the heart.

Or take the businessman who submits an honest expense report but feels cheated by his employer. He wouldn't steal, but he daydreams about ways to cut corners. He imagines a scenario where he pads an expense just a little, thinking, "It's not like I'm robbing them." He never does it, but in his heart, he has already justified compromise.

Then there's the Christian woman scrolling through social media. She sees a post about someone she secretly dislikes. Outwardly, she never says a negative word. But inside, she takes pleasure in their failure. She reads every negative comment, nodding along in silent agreement. No one sees it, but God does.

A churchgoer might be known for doing everything right. He tithes, he serves, he never curses, drinks, or does anything scandalous. But if you could see inside his mind, it would tell a different story. He secretly looks down on others who don't meet his standards. He is filled with pride, comparing himself to those around him. On the outside, he looks holy, but on the inside, he is far from God.

Or think about the believer who is driving in traffic. Someone cuts him off, and he holds back from honking or yelling. But in his mind, he lets loose, imagining himself putting that driver in their place. He might even replay the moment for the rest of the day, fueling frustration over something that happened in seconds. He didn't sin outwardly, but his heart was consumed with anger.

Jesus didn't come just to clean up our behavior. He came to change our hearts.

Proverbs 4:23 says, *"Above all else, guard your heart, for everything you do flows from it."* If we want to live set apart, we must take inventory of our thoughts. The first step is filling our minds with God's Word. The more we dwell on truth, the less room there is for toxic thoughts. **Philippians 4:8** tells us to think on things that are true, noble, right, pure, lovely, and admirable. When our minds are filled with these things, there is no space for thoughts that lead us away from God.

We also have to take every thought captive. 2 Corinthians 10:5 says we must *"take every thought captive to obey Christ."* We can't always control what thoughts come, but we can decide what we entertain. Not every thought deserves a seat at the table. Some need to be cast out immediately.

David understood this when he prayed,

> *Create in me a clean heart, O God, and renew a right spirit within me"*
> **Psalm 51:10**

We don't purify ourselves. God does. But we must invite Him in. We must ask Him to transform not just our actions but our desires, our motives, and our thoughts.

Being set apart isn't just about what we do. It's about who we are at the core. God calls us to purity, not just in action, but in thought. And when we allow Him to transform our minds, our lives will follow.

If God looks at the heart, then so should we. The way we think about others matters just as much as the way we think about ourselves. First Samuel 16:7 says, *"For the Lord sees not as man sees: man looks on the outward appearance, but the Lord looks on the heart."* That verse reminds us that while the world judges people based on how they look, what they wear, or what they have, God is only concerned with who they truly are inside.

It is so easy to size people up at first glance. We might assume things about someone because of their clothing, their background, or their lifestyle. We might even think we know their spiritual condition just by looking at them. But Jesus never judged people that way. He saw past the outward shell and looked straight into the heart. He saw Zacchaeus, not as a greedy tax collector, but as a man who was searching for redemption. He saw the woman at the well, not as a sinner to be shunned, but as someone longing for truth.

When we judge people by appearances, we miss what God is doing in their lives. Maybe the man covered in tattoos sitting at the back of the church is closer to God than the man in a suit sitting on the front row. Maybe the young woman struggling with addiction is one prayer away from freedom, while the person who looks like they have it all together is barely hanging on. We should try to see what God sees, and that is why we must be careful not to let our minds create barriers that God never intended.

The way we think about others affects how we treat them. If we assume the worst about someone, we will struggle to love them the way Jesus does. But if we choose to see people through the eyes of grace, we will extend the same mercy that God has given to us. Instead of focusing on what is wrong with others, we should pray that God helps us see them the way He does.

In the same way that we are called to keep our own hearts pure, we are also called to look at others with pure hearts. **James 2:1** warns, *"My brothers, show no partiality as you hold the faith in our Lord Jesus Christ, the Lord of glory."* We must resist the temptation to elevate some people while looking down on others. God does not judge by outward appearances, and neither should we.

When we allow God to transform our minds, it changes everything. It changes how we think about sin, how we think about ourselves, and how we think about others. Instead of just trying to be good, we actually become good from the inside out. Instead of focusing on appearances, we see people the way God sees them. And when our hearts align with His, our lives will truly reflect His holiness.

It's what's inside that counts.

HEART CHECK

God isn't impressed by outward appearances, He looks at the heart. True transformation starts on the inside, long before it shows on the outside.

- ✝ Are there thoughts, motives, or attitudes you've ignored because they aren't visible to others?
- ✝ Have you been more focused on looking good outwardly rather than being pure inwardly?
- ✝ How do you see others? Do you judge by appearances, or do you ask God to help you see them through His eyes?

Pray and Believe: Ask God to search your heart and reveal anything that doesn't align with Him. Pray:

"Lord, create in me a clean heart. Transform my thoughts, my motives, and my desires so that my life truly reflects You from the inside out."

It's not just about what you do, it's about who you are becoming. Let God shape you from the heart.

CHAPTER 9

HUMILITY PRECEDES HONOR

The path to true honor isn't found in self-promotion or striving for recognition. It comes through surrender, service, and trust. Proverbs 18:12 reminds us, *"Before destruction the heart of a man is haughty, and before honor is humility."* In God's kingdom, the way up always starts by going down. Humility isn't something our world naturally values. Society pushes us to fight for our place, demand respect, and make sure we aren't overlooked. But in God's kingdom, honor isn't something we take, it's something He gives. Jesus taught,

> *Whoever exalts himself will be humbled, and he who humbles himself will be exalted"*
>
> **Matthew 23:12**

God consistently works through those who walk in humility.

If you're in a season where you feel unseen or undervalued, this truth is for you: God hasn't forgotten you. He's preparing you. And when the time is right, He will lift you up in ways beyond what you could imagine.

Humility is often misunderstood. It doesn't mean thinking less of yourself, it means thinking of yourself less. It's not weakness; it's controlled strength. A humble person doesn't have low self-worth, nor do they shy away from their calling. Instead, they walk with quiet confidence, knowing their value comes from God, not the approval of others.

Jesus modeled humility perfectly. **Philippians 2:5-9** describes it this way: *"Let this mind be in you which was also in Christ Jesus, who, being in the form of God, did not consider it robbery to be equal with God, but made Himself of no reputation, taking the form of a servant, and coming in the likeness of men. And* *being found in appearance as a man, He humbled Himself and became obedient to the point of death, even the death of the cross. Therefore God also has highly exalted Him and given Him the name which is above every name."* Jesus, who had every right to claim honor and glory, chose instead to serve. He washed His disciples' feet.

He spent time with the broken. He didn't chase recognition, yet God exalted Him above all. If Jesus embraced humility before glory, how much more should we?

If humility leads to honor, pride leads to destruction. Pride deceives us into believing we must take control, push ourselves forward, and make things happen on our own. It whispers that waiting on God is foolish and that we should create our own success. But **Proverbs 16:18** warns, *"Pride goes before destruction, and a haughty spirit before a fall."* King Nebuchadnezzar's story in Daniel 4 is a perfect example. He was the most powerful man of his time, ruling over the vast Babylonian Empire. One day, as he stood on the rooftop of his palace, he looked over the city and said, *"Is not this great Babylon, that I have built for a royal dwelling by my mighty power and for the honor of my majesty?"* **(See Daniel 4:30)**. The moment he took credit for his success, his downfall began. God humbled him, stripping him of his kingdom and even his sanity. He wandered like an animal, eating grass, until he finally looked up and acknowledged that God alone is sovereign. Only then was his honor restored.

Pride isn't always loud and obvious. Sometimes, it's subtle, slipping into our hearts in ways we don't immediately recognize. It doesn't always look like arrogance or boastfulness; more often, it takes on quieter forms, slowly shaping our thoughts, attitudes, and actions.

Here are a few way pride can show up in our life:

- ✞ **Self-Sufficiency:** It is the belief that we can handle things on our own and don't really need God in our daily decisions. Instead of seeking His guidance, we rely on our own wisdom, only turning to Him when things go wrong.

- ✞ **Unwillingness To Admit When We Are Wrong:** When we get defensive, shift blame, or justify our actions instead of humbling ourselves and taking responsibility it prevents us from asking for forgiveness and from making amends when we've hurt someone. It makes us hold tightly to our opinions, refusing correction because we don't want to appear weak or uninformed.

- ✞ **Comparison:** This form of pride makes us jealous of others' success or dissatisfied with our own lives. Instead of celebrating others, we silently wonder why we weren't the ones recognized, promoted, or blessed. It shifts our focus away from gratitude and toward resentment, as if we are competing for God's favor rather than trusting that He has a unique plan for each of us.

- ✞ **Judgemental Spirit:** A judgmental spirit leads us to criticize others for their mistakes while excusing our own. We become quick to point out flaws, failures, or shortcomings in others without considering our own need for grace. It blinds us to our faults and makes us feel superior, forgetting that we, too, are in constant need of God's mercy.

- ✞ **Entitlement:** This subtle yet dangerous form of pride tells us that we deserve better than what we have, and that we've earned a certain status, recognition, or comfort. When things don't go our way, pride makes us frustrated and bitter instead of grateful for what we've already been given. Entitlement causes us to approach life with an attitude of demand rather than appreciation.

- **False Humility:** When we downplay our abilities, deflect compliments, or pretend to be less capable than we are, we might think we're being humble. But true humility isn't about making ourselves appear small, it's about shifting the focus away from ourselves entirely. False humility still keeps the attention on us, making our insecurity just another form of pride.

Pride, in all its forms, slowly distances us from God. It hardens our hearts, makes us resistant to change, and blinds us to our own need for grace. Recognizing it is the first step toward true humility, allowing us to surrender our hearts to God and trust Him to shape us into who He's called us to be. The biggest danger of pride is that it distances us from God. **James 4:6** says, *"God resists the proud, but gives grace to the humble."* When pride takes root in our hearts, we become less receptive to God's leading, less willing to change, and less aware of our need for Him.

Humility isn't just an attitude; it's something that should be visible in our daily lives. It's not just about avoiding pride but actively choosing to humble ourselves in practical ways.

Walking in humility requires intentionality and a willingness to put others before ourselves, even in the smallest moments. One of the clearest signs of humility is the ability to admit when we're wrong. It's rarely easy, especially when we feel justified, but taking responsibility for our mistakes opens the door to healing. Whether it's with a spouse, a friend, a coworker, or even a stranger, saying, *"I was wrong, and I'm sorry,"* can break down walls of pride. A humble person doesn't make excuses or shift blame, they own their actions.

Pride tells us we have all the answers, but humility keeps us teachable. Seeking advice and truly listening to others is a simple but powerful way to practice humility. Whether it's asking for counsel from a mentor, listening to a friend's perspective without interrupting, or being open to correction from a leader, a humble heart remains willing to learn.

Arguments often drag on because of pride. We want the last word. We want to prove our point. But humility means knowing when to let go, even if we believe we're right. Choosing peace over proving ourselves to be correct is a true act of humility. It requires us to lay down our pride, resist the urge to defend ourselves, and instead seek unity over division. When we surrender our need to prove a point, we make space for God to work in ways our arguments never could. True humility doesn't mean we ignore truth, but it does mean we value love and understanding more than winning a debate. In the end, choosing peace not only honors God, but it also strengthens our character and deepens our faith.

One of the best ways to practice humility is through service, especially in unseen ways. For example, Jesus washed His disciples' feet, taking on the role of a servant. In our daily lives, humility looks like serving without expecting recognition. It's doing household chores without being asked, covering a shift for a coworker, picking up trash that isn't yours, or helping someone in need without making a big deal about it. A humble heart doesn't serve for applause, it serves out of love.

Pride makes us compare ourselves to others, which leads to jealousy when someone else succeeds. But humility allows us to celebrate others instead of competing with them. The next time a coworker gets the promotion you wanted, a friend receives an opportunity you prayed for, or someone else is praised while you are overlooked, choose to celebrate them. The ability to lift others up, even when we feel unseen, is a powerful act of humility. In fact, I have never seen such a time when so many people refuse to celebrate the success of others. Maybe I'm just wired differently, but when I see other people throw a touchdown I want to celebrate with them, not down-play their success. We should all want others to succeed as much as, or even more than, ourselves.

True humility gives without expecting anything in return. Whether it's paying for a stranger's meal, helping an elderly neighbor with yard work, writing an encouraging note, or volunteering, the less recognition we seek for our kindness, the more humility grows in us. Jesus said, *"For whoever exalts himself will be humbled, and he who humbles himself will be exalted"* **(See Luke 14:11).** He taught that we shouldn't seek the best seats at a banquet but should take the lowest place instead. This might mean doing the job no one else wants, staying behind to clean up after an event, or letting someone else take the spotlight. Humility doesn't need to be seen, it finds joy in serving from the background.

Pride clings to offense, demanding justice, but humility lets things go. Forgiving someone, even when they don't apologize, is an act of surrender to God. Holding onto bitterness keeps us stuck, but choosing to forgive allows us to walk in freedom. Pride says, *"I deserve this."* Humility says, *"I am grateful and blessed to have this."* A grateful heart is a humble heart, recognizing that everything we have is a gift from God.

Humility isn't something we master once and for all, it's a daily choice. Asking God to help us remain humble, to reveal areas of pride in our hearts, and to give us opportunities to serve others keeps us on the right path. When we continually surrender to Him, He shapes us into people He can use for His glory. If you're in a season where you feel unseen or overlooked, take heart, God is at work. He sees every act of humility, every unseen moment of service, and every sacrifice you make.

Keep serving. Keep trusting. Keep walking in humility. And in His perfect timing, He will honor you in ways far beyond what you could imagine.

HEART CHECK

Pride is subtle. It doesn't always announce itself loudly, it often hides in small thoughts, quiet justifications, and unnoticed attitudes. But God sees beyond actions; He searches the heart. Humility begins when we allow Him to reveal what's inside.

- ✝ Have you been relying more on your own strength and wisdom rather than seeking God daily?
- ✝ Do you struggle to admit when you're wrong, holding onto your pride instead of pursuing reconciliation?
- ✝ When others succeed, do you feel genuine joy for them, or does jealousy quietly creep in?
- ✝ Are you more focused on receiving recognition than serving from a place of love?
- ✝ Do you judge others for their shortcomings while excusing your own?

Pray and Believe: Ask God to expose any pride in your heart and replace it with humility. Pray:

"Lord, search my heart and reveal any pride that keeps me from fully surrendering to You. Teach me to serve without seeking attention, to celebrate others without comparison, and to trust Your timing instead of forcing my own way. Help me embrace humility as Jesus did, knowing that true honor comes from You alone."

Humility isn't weakness; it's the strength to trust God completely. Let Him shape you from the inside out.

CHAPTER 10

TRUSTING THE ARCHITECT

There is a beautiful truth that can anchor our souls through every high and low of life: it is the fact that God has a plan for your life. It is not a vague, uncertain plan, but a perfect, purposeful design created by the One who knows us better than we know ourselves. Life often throws us into seasons of uncertainty and volatility where nothing makes sense, making it easy to wonder if we have been forgotten. But, the God we serve is not a God of confusion. He is the God of order, direction, and intentionality. His plans are good, even if they do not feel good in the moment. His ways are higher than ours, His thoughts beyond our understanding, yet He invites us to trust Him every step of the way. His plan does not waver based on our circumstances. Even in the moments when we feel like everything is falling apart, He is weaving something beautiful behind the scenes, something that we may not fully understand until later.

Trusting God's plan is one of the most challenging aspects of faith because we often want control over our own lives. If we are honest, most of us prefer to know the full roadmap before we even take the first step. We want to be certain of every detail before we commit to the journey. But faith requires trust in the unseen. God's plan often unfolds like the pages of a book. We do not get to read the last chapter before we finish the first. If we did, it would not be faith at all. Our journey requires patience and confidence that God is directing our paths, even when we cannot see the outcome. The more we walk with Him, the more we begin to understand that He is always working behind the scenes. He is orchestrating details we may not recognize until much later, but He is never idle. We may not always understand why He allows certain things, but we can trust that He is always working for our good. Even when doors close, when opportunities pass, or when the road takes an unexpected turn, God is not caught off guard. He is putting together something far greater than we could imagine. He is carefully aligning circumstances in ways we would have never thought of, to produce an outcome that we never would have seen coming.

The Bible is filled with stories that reveal how God's plan often unfolds in ways that seem confusing at first, yet lead to something far greater than anyone could have foreseen. Abraham was called to leave everything he knew and go to a place he had never seen. There were no maps, no details, only a promise. Abraham obeyed, even though he did not know where he was going. That level of trust in God's plan is certainly something we all can aspire to. Many times, God will ask us to take only single steps before without revealing the destination. His plan requires faith, not full visibility. Following God with faith is like driving with headlights in the dark. They do not illuminate the entire road, only a short distance ahead. Yet that light is enough to keep us moving forward. We may not see every twist, turn, or challenge that lies ahead, but as long as we trust the path and keep going, we will reach our destination. Just as a driver relies on the light that is directly in front of them, we rely on faith to guide us step by step, knowing that what we cannot see now will be revealed in time.

Joseph's life is a stunning example of how God's plan includes detours. Betrayed by his brothers, sold into slavery, falsely accused, and thrown into prison, everything seemed to be falling apart. But God was positioning him for a greater purpose. When Joseph finally saw how it all came together, he told his brothers that what they intended for harm, God intended for good. How often do we question the trials we face, only to look back later and see how God was using those moments for something greater?

Moses did not see himself as a leader, yet God called him to free His people. Even after his obedience, delays in the wilderness made it seem like the promise would never come to pass. But every step, every delay, was part of God's divine process. Just because the promise is delayed does not mean it is denied.

> *For the vision is yet for an appointed time, but at the end it shall speak, and not lie: though it tarry, wait for it; because it will surely come, it will not tarry."*
> **Habakkuk 2:3**

We often want answers right away, but God works in seasons, not in hurried moments.

Undoubtedly, there are moments in life when we feel lost, abandoned, or confused. We pray, but the answer does not come. We knock, but the doors remain closed. It is in these moments that we must remember that God is not absent. He is working. He is aligning things beyond what we can see. The promise that all things work together for good for those who love God and are called according to His purpose is something we can hold onto. **(See Romans 8:28)** *"All things"* means the good and the bad. The heartbreak, the loss, the disappointments, they are not wasted. God is using them to shape us, refine us, and prepare us for what is ahead. The moments that feel like setbacks are often setups for something greater. We must hold onto the truth that God sees the entire picture, while we see only a fraction of what is really happening.

Waiting is one of the hardest aspects of trusting God's plan. We live in a world that values speed, but God's kingdom operates on a different timetable. His timing is perfect, even when it feels slow. We often want immediate results, but God is more concerned with our growth than the speed of our arrival. Sometimes, He allows delays because He is doing something deeper in us. He is building our faith, preparing our hearts, and setting things in motion that we cannot yet see. He does not rush what He is perfecting. When we feel like we are waiting too long, it's good to remind ourselves that God's timing is never wrong. He knows what is best for us, and He knows when we are ready to step into the next phase of His plan.

Trusting God's plan means surrendering control. It means acknowledging that we do not have all the answers, but we trust the One who does. This is not always easy, but it is always worth it. If God started something in us, He will finish it. **(See Philippians 1:6)** He does not abandon His children. He does not forget His promises. He is faithful to complete what He begins.

How do we recognize God's plan? It starts with seeking Him. The Lord makes firm the steps of the one who delights in Him. **(See Psalm 37:23)** Practical ways to discern His plan include prayer, asking God for direction and wisdom, aligning our decisions with Scripture, listening for the Holy Spirit's guidance, and seeking Godly mentors. God does not want us to wander aimlessly. He leads those who seek Him. The more we lean into Him, the clearer our steps will become.

However, fear often keeps us from embracing God's plan. We worry about the unknown, about failure, about what others will think. But fear has no place in a heart that trusts God. He has not given us a spirit of fear, but of power, love, and a sound mind. **(See 2 Timothy 1:7)** Stepping into God's plan requires courage, but He goes with us every step of the way. He does not call us into something just to leave us to figure it out on our own. Whatever you are facing, know this, God has a plan. It may not look the way you expected, but it is good. It is purposeful. And He will be faithful to bring it to completion. Trust Him. Walk by faith. And watch His beautiful plan unfold in your life.

HEART CHECK

✞ Are there areas of your life where you struggle to surrender control to God?

✞ Have you been impatient, wanting answers immediately rather than trusting His perfect timing?

✞ Do you find yourself questioning whether God is truly working in your situation?

✞ Are you allowing fear to hold you back from stepping fully into God's plan?

Pray and Believe: Ask God to strengthen your trust in Him and to help you surrender your worries to Him. Remind yourself that He sees what you cannot and is working all things together for your good. Trust Him, walk by faith, and embrace His perfect plan for your life.

CHAPTER 11

CLOSER

> *Draw near to God, and He will draw near to you."*
> **James 4:8**

There is a longing inside every believer for something deeper, something more. We know there is more to this walk of faith than simply going through the motions. Deep in our spirit, we crave closeness with God, our creator. The good news is that He desires the same thing. In fact, that's how he designed us. When we were created there was an emptiness left on the inside that only He could fill. This emptiness makes us crave a relationship with him. It makes us long to be closer to Him.

The closer we get to Him, the more we find that He is the answer to every challenge we could ever face. We discover that it is only God who holds the answer to the questions we have. He is not a distant figure that is far removed from our lives. He is a loving Father who desires to be involved in every detail of our journey. I've heard people say things like, "I don't want to pray about something so little, God has bigger things to deal with." Nonsense. That is tantamount to believing that God answers our prayers because He owes us something or is repaying a favor, causing us to wait until we have a big need instead of seeking Him in the small things. He is deeply interested in every facet of your life, you just have to make the first move toward him. Not the other way around. We all must realize that God made the first move towards us by giving his son Jesus. Now it's our turn.

Drawing closer to God requires intentionality on our part. It requires a heart that is fully devoted and set apart for Him. Many believers struggle to maintain a deep connection with God because they have not fully embraced the call to consecration. Yet, consecration is the key to experiencing a relationship with God that is rich, fulfilling, and transformational.

John Wesley, a prominent 18th-century theologian and preacher, described consecration as *"giving yourselves wholly to Him who gave Himself wholly for you. Consecrate all your words, thoughts, and actions to His glory. Let your heart, your will, your affections, and your whole being be devoted to God."*

God does not want a distant relationship. He calls us to be set apart, fully devoted to Him. Consecration is not about rules or restrictions, but about love and intimacy. It is the act of giving ourselves completely to God, making Him the highest priority in our lives. When we consecrate ourselves, we remove distractions and lesser things so that we can give Him our full attention. We choose Him above all else.

Throughout Scripture, we see the power of consecration. Moses met with God face to face because he set himself apart. He left behind the comforts of Egypt, choosing instead to seek the presence of God on Mount Sinai. Daniel remained steadfast in his devotion despite living in a pagan culture. He refused to defile himself with the king's food, choosing instead to honor God. Paul laid everything down to pursue Christ above all else. He considered all his past accomplishments as nothing compared to the surpassing greatness of knowing Jesus.

These men knew the secret to a victorious life. They understood that consecration was not a burden, but a blessing. It was not about loss, but about gain. The closer they were to God, the more they experienced His power, wisdom, and guidance.

Many things can keep us from drawing near to God. Sin, distractions, and even our own pride can build barriers between us and the One who loves us most. We may not even realize that we have drifted until we find ourselves feeling distant, overwhelmed, and spiritually dry. But true closeness comes through surrender. When we let go of control and trust Him fully, we experience His peace and guidance in ways we never imagined.

I love to tell the story of how I once shared with a pastor friend that my journey into consecration saved my life. I had been weighed down by poor mindsets, my focus was scattered, and my relationship with God was growing colder by the day. Then, everything changed when I heard a sermon that deeply impacted me. A well-known pastor described his daily morning practice, explaining how he prayed, read, and meditated on God's Word every single morning without fail.

"That's it!" I thought to myself. That was the missing piece. My journey found new life that day. From that moment on, I committed to starting every day with God, no matter the circumstances. Rain or shine, workday or vacation, I made it my priority. My wife and I already give the first fruits of our income, so why not give the first portion of my time as well? I had no idea what I had been missing out on.

Since then, I have made it a daily practice to spend my mornings in prayer, Bible study, thanksgiving, interceding for others, and sitting in quietness with God. Without hesitation, I can say it was the best decision I have ever made regarding how I spend my time.

However, surrender is not always easy. Our human nature resists it. We want to be in control, to hold onto our plans, and to navigate life on our own terms. But true intimacy with God requires us to lay everything at His feet. It requires us to let go of our fears, our ambitions, and our desires, trusting that He knows what is best.

Consider Abraham. He was willing to sacrifice Isaac because he trusted God completely. His surrender led to God's miraculous provision. When we surrender, we position ourselves to see God move powerfully in our lives. When we release our grip on the things we hold most dear, we find that God is faithful to lead us into His perfect will.

Difficult times have a way of either drawing us closer to God or pulling us away from Him. When life is hard, we are faced with a choice. We can allow our trials to push us into His arms, seeking His strength and guidance, or we can let them create distance, allowing doubt and fear to take root. The difference lies in our response. Those who choose to draw near to the fire experience a depth of relationship with God that cannot be found in times of ease.

Look at how Job endured unimaginable loss. He lost his family, his health, and his possessions, yet he refused to turn away. Though his suffering was great, his trust in God never wavered. Then there's David, a man after God's own heart, faced relentless battles, betrayal, and hardship. Through it all, he continually sought the Lord. His psalms reveal a man who turned to God in every season, whether in moments of triumph or in the depths of despair.

These men remind us that trials are not meant to destroy our faith but to deepen it. When we choose to lean into God rather than pull away, we find that He is always near, refining us, strengthening us, and drawing us closer than ever before.

God does not waste our struggles. Every trial is an opportunity to grow in faith and dependence on Him. The fire refines us, removing what is unnecessary and making us more like Christ. It burns away selfishness, pride, and anything that hinders our closeness with Him. If we let Him, God will use every hardship to bring us closer than we have ever been before.

A close relationship with God is not just for Sunday mornings or desperate moments. It is a daily journey. We grow closer to Him through simple, consistent habits. Prayer, worship, studying Scripture, and listening for His voice are not religious obligations but pathways to intimacy. Just as relationships with people require time and effort, so does our relationship with God.

Closeness with God is built in the small moments. When we wake up and choose to spend time with Him, when we worship in the car, when we pray throughout the day, we cultivate intimacy with Him. It is not about perfection but about pursuit. He meets us where we are when we seek Him with all our hearts.

Being set apart for God is not just about what we avoid, but about what we pursue. A consecrated life is a life of purpose. When we walk closely with God, our lives become marked by His presence. He reveals His plans for us and equips us to fulfill them. We do not have to struggle to find meaning in life. When we stay close to Him, our purpose becomes clear.

However, the greatest reward of drawing near to God is simply knowing Him. Everything else, including peace, wisdom, strength, and joy, is a byproduct of intimacy with Him. When we make Him our first love, we find that He is truly all we need, or could ever desire.

There is no situation too difficult, no burden too heavy, and no heartache too deep that closeness with God cannot heal. The solution to every problem is not found in striving but in abiding. When we stay close to Him, we will never be without direction, comfort, or hope. So draw near. Consecrate your life to Him. Let go of distractions and seek Him with all your heart. He is waiting, ready to draw close to you in return. And, when you find yourself in His presence, you will discover that closeness with Him is the greatest treasure of all.

HEART CHECK

- ✞ Do you sense a longing for deeper intimacy with God, but struggle to make time for Him?
- ✞ Are there distractions or habits in your life that are keeping you from fully consecrating yourself to Him?
- ✞ Do you bring both the big and small details of your life to God in prayer, or do you sometimes hold back?
- ✞ Have you resisted surrendering certain areas of your life, fearing what it might cost you?
- ✞ Are trials drawing you closer to God, or are they creating distance between you and Him?

Pray and Believe: Ask God to reveal any areas where you need to draw closer to Him. Surrender distractions, fears, and anything that keeps you from fully consecrating your life to Him. Pray for a heart that seeks Him first, not out of obligation, but out of love. Trust that as you draw near, He will meet you with His presence, wisdom, and peace. Choose today to pursue closeness with Him above all else.

CHAPTER 12

TIMES OF REFRESHING

Times of refreshing come from the presence of the Lord. This is not just a promise, but a reality for every believer who turns their heart fully toward Him. Life has a way of draining us. We go through seasons where we feel dry, weary, and distant from God. We press forward, but our strength feels depleted. It is in those moments that God invites us into something deeper, something life-giving. He calls us to Himself so that He can renew our spirit and pour out fresh wind upon our souls. **Acts 3:19** says, "Repent, then, and turn to God, so that your sins may be wiped out, that times of refreshing may come from the Lord." The key to refreshment is not found in more effort, but in turning back to the presence of God, where everything we need is waiting for us.

A dry season does not mean God has left you. It does not mean you are failing. It simply means you need the refreshing that only He can bring. Imagine a land scorched by the sun, cracked and barren, longing for rain.

When the first drops begin to fall, the ground drinks it in, and before long, life springs up where there was once only dust. This is exactly what happens in our spiritual lives when we allow the presence of God to rain down on us. What was lifeless comes alive again. What felt hopeless begins to thrive. Some of us have been running on empty for too long, trying to push through exhaustion, discouragement, or even routine faith. But God does not want us just to survive. He wants us to be renewed.

Spiritual dryness happens when we drift away from our source. Sometimes we do not even realize how far we have wandered. We get caught up in responsibilities, distractions, or struggles, and before we know it, we are distant from the very presence that sustains us; from the very source of our life. When we are not drawing from God's presence, we start running on our own strength, and that strength runs out quickly. The good news is that God is not waiting to scold us. He is waiting to refresh us. He invites us to turn back, not in shame, but in expectation. He is always ready to restore and breathe new life into weary hearts.

Acts 3:19 is an invitation to turn toward God and experience renewal. This is not just about repentance from sin, though that is part of it. It is about shifting our focus back to Him. It is about positioning ourselves under the flow of His Spirit so that we can receive what we need. Times of refreshing do not come from striving harder or trying to fix everything ourselves. They come from being with Him. Just like the fresh wind of revival sweeps over a church or a city, His Spirit wants to sweep through your heart. He wants to lift the weight you have been carrying, replace your weariness with strength, and awaken your spirit with His presence.

True refreshment is only found in God's presence. The world offers distractions, temporary escapes, and quick fixes, but nothing truly restores like time with the Lord. When you are spiritually dry, the best thing you can do is run to Him. Jesus said in **Matthew 11:28**, *"Come to me, all who are weary and burdened, and I will give you rest."* This is more than physical rest. It is soul-deep renewal. It is the kind of peace that quiets the storm inside you. It is the "my cup runneth over" kind of restoration that revives your joy. It's the kind of fresh wind that fills your sails again and propels you forward.

There are seasons when God calls us to stillness so He can refresh us. Sometimes, we resist that stillness because we equate movement with progress. But God often does His greatest work in us when we simply stop and surrender. His presence does more for us in one moment than all our efforts combined. Renewal is not about earning something. It is about receiving what He is freely giving. He is the well that never runs dry, the living water that restores our souls. If you are weary, if you feel distant, if you are longing for a fresh touch from God, He is ready to pour out His Spirit on you.

If you want to walk in daily renewal, you have to stay connected to your source. Make time for His presence. Let worship and prayer become your place of refreshing. Surround yourself with people who stir up your faith rather than drain your spirit. Release the burdens that are not yours to carry and trust that God is working even when you do not see it. A heart that stays near to Him will never stay dry for long.

God is not done with you. He is not going to leave you in this dry place. He is sending fresh wind. He is stirring revival in your heart. He is pouring out times of refreshing, and all you have to do is turn toward Him and receive it. What was weary is about to be strengthened. What was empty is about to be filled. What felt distant is about to be drawn close again. There is no need to keep pushing forward in your own strength when His presence is ready to restore you. The fresh wind of His Spirit is here. Breathe it in. Step into His presence. Let Him renew you, because times of refreshing are waiting.

HEART CHECK

- ✝ Have I been feeling spiritually dry or distant from God?
- ✝ Am I running on my own strength instead of relying on God's presence to refresh me?
- ✝ Have I allowed distractions, busyness, or discouragement to pull me away from time with Him?
- ✝ Do I truly believe that God wants to restore and renew me?
- ✝ Have I made space in my life for God to pour out fresh wind into my spirit?
- ✝ Am I carrying burdens that I need to release into His hands?
- ✝ Do I regularly seek time in worship, prayer, and the Word as my source of renewal?
- ✝ What is one step I can take today to receive the refreshing that God has for me?

Pray and Believe: "Lord, I come to You in need of refreshing. I lay down my weariness, distractions, and anything that has pulled me away from Your presence. Fill me with fresh wind. Renew my heart, restore my joy, and draw me close to You again. I trust that You are the source of true refreshment, and I receive it now. Thank You for always being near and for never leaving me in a dry place. In Jesus' name, Amen."

Take a moment to reflect. What is one step you can take today to draw near to God and receive His spirit of refreshing? Write it down and move forward in faith.

CHAPTER 13

THE WAY BACK HOME

The way back home is never as far as it feels. Life has a way of pulling people away from faith, sometimes slowly and almost without notice, other times through pain, disappointment, or even rebellion. One day you wake up and realize you are not where you used to be with God. The closeness you once felt has faded. Your prayers are rare, or maybe they do not come at all. Worship feels distant. Church feels unfamiliar or even unwelcoming. The guilt or shame of drifting away starts to weigh heavy, and the question arises, "Can I really come back?" The answer is yes. Without hesitation, without conditions, and without earning your way back. God's arms are open, and His heart has never stopped longing for you.

Distance from God rarely happens in a single moment. Most of the time it is a slow drift. You get caught up in responsibilities, struggles, or distractions, and before you know it, faith is no longer central. For others, it may be tied to a deep wound, a season of doubt, or a moment of rebellion. Maybe life threw something at you that you did not expect, and it shook your faith. Maybe prayers felt unanswered, and you wondered if God was really listening. Perhaps people who claimed to represent God left you hurt, disappointed, or betrayed.

Whatever the reason, you found yourself away from Him, and now there is something stirring inside of you, a longing to return but uncertainty about how to do it.

If that is where you are, I want you to know that you are not alone. And more importantly, you are not too far gone. God's heart toward you is not filled with anger or disappointment. It is filled with love. If you need proof, look at the story Jesus told about the prodigal son. This was a young man who deliberately left his father's house, took everything he had, wasted it all, and ended up in the lowest possible place. He had nothing left and thought he would have to return in shame and beg to be a servant in his father's house. But when he started the journey home, his father saw him from a distance and ran to meet him. Not with anger. Not with punishment, but with open arms, joy, and full restoration. That is the heart of God toward you.

Coming back to God does not require you to have everything figured out. It does not require a perfectly crafted prayer or a flawless plan to fix what has been broken. It starts with a simple step, a turning of your heart back toward Him. Maybe that step is a whispered prayer after a long time of silence. Maybe it is opening the Bible again and reading the words of Jesus. Maybe it is stepping back into a church even when it feels unfamiliar.

The most important thing is that you move toward Him, because the moment you do, He is already running toward you.

There will always be barriers that try to keep you from taking that step. Shame will tell you that you have been gone too long and that God is disappointed in you. Fear will whisper that others will judge you if you return.

Doubt will make you question whether God is really as loving and forgiving as He says He is. The enemy will do everything he can to convince you that it is too late, that you have made too many mistakes, or that God has moved on. But those are lies. The truth is that Jesus already made the way for you to come back, and nothing you have done has changed His love for you.

When you return to God, it is not about going backward. It is about moving forward into the life He has for you. Faith is a journey, and restoration is not about perfection but about walking daily in relationship with Him.

There will be days when you feel strong and close to Him, and there will be days when you struggle. That is okay. What matters is that you keep coming back, that you keep showing up, that you keep trusting that His grace is enough. You do not have to earn His love. It has been waiting for you all along.

No matter how far you feel, the way home is always open. God is not standing at a distance with crossed arms waiting to see if you can prove yourself. He is watching for you with joy, ready to embrace you and remind you that you belong. The door has never been locked. The light has never been turned off. Home is still home, and you are still His. All you have to do is take the first step. He will meet you there.

HEART CHECK

- ✞ Have I felt distant from God but unsure how to come back?
- ✞ What has caused me to drift away; is it busyness, hurt, doubt, disappointment, or something else?
- ✞ Do I believe the lie that I have gone too far for God to welcome me back?
- ✞ What fears or hesitations are holding me back from fully returning to Him?
- ✞ Am I willing to take the first step, even if I do not have all the answers?
- ✞ Do I trust that God is not waiting to condemn me but to restore and embrace me?
- ✞ What is one practical way I can move toward God today?

Pray and Believe: *"Lord, I come to You with a heart that longs to return. I lay down my fears, doubts, and shame, knowing that Your love for me has never changed. Thank You for always keeping the way open and for running toward me when I turn to You. I surrender the things that have kept me distant and ask for Your grace to renew and restore me. Help me to trust that I am fully forgiven, fully loved, and always welcome in Your presence. In Jesus' name, Amen."*

Take a moment to reflect. What is the first step you can take today to draw near to God? Write it down, pray over it, and move forward in faith. Home is waiting.

CHAPTER 14

THE COURAGE TO BE WHO GOD CREATED YOU TO BE

The courage to be who God created you to be is one of the greatest challenges and one of the most important victories in the life of a believer. Every person is born with a unique purpose, crafted by the hands of a loving Creator who makes no mistakes. Yet, so many of us struggle to fully embrace that identity. We shrink back, questioning if we are enough, often wondering if we should be more like someone else, trying to fit into a mold that was never meant for us. But God did not create you to be someone else. He created you to be exactly who He designed, on purpose and for a purpose.

Fear has a way of whispering lies that can feel louder than truth. It tells you that you are not good enough, that you are too much or not enough, that you are inadequate or incapable. Fear wants you to believe that your past disqualifies you or that your weaknesses define you. The enemy loves to use comparison and insecurity to keep you from stepping into the fullness of what God has planned. But fear is a liar. God's Word makes it clear that you were not given a spirit of fear but of power, love, and a sound mind. **(See 2 Timothy 1:7)** When you begin to see yourself through the eyes of your Creator instead of the expectations of the world, you realize that your value and purpose were never based on your own abilities. They were established by the One who formed you.

God did not make a mistake when He created you. Every gift, every personality trait, every experience, and even every struggle has been woven together into a design that serves a purpose beyond what you can see. Psalm 139 reminds us that we are fearfully and wonderfully made, knit together in our mother's womb with intentionality and love. Yet, so often, we fight against that design. It's easy to wish we were different. We try to hide parts of ourselves that feel inconvenient. We let the opinions of others shape who we become instead of trusting the One who created us. The truth is, you will never find peace trying to be something you were never meant to be. Peace comes when you embrace who God made you to be and walk in that identity with confidence.

Comparison is one of the greatest thieves of joy. It convinces you to measure yourself against others, making you feel like you are always coming up short. But God never intended for you to be a copy of someone else. He has given you a specific calling, and the more you try to be like someone else, the more you rob the world of the unique gift that is you. The Bible tells us that we are not called to seek the approval of man but of God. **(See Galations 1:10)** If we live for the approval of others, we will always feel like we are falling short. But when we focus on living for an audience of One, we walk in a freedom that cannot be shaken by opinions, criticism, or comparison.

It takes faith to walk boldly in your God-given identity. It takes courage to trust that God's plan is better than any version of success the world offers. There are moments when stepping into that calling will feel like stepping out of a boat onto uncertain waters, just like Peter when Jesus called him to walk on the waves. But bold faith is not about having all the answers. It is about keeping your eyes on the One who called you. It is about trusting that if God designed you with a purpose, He will also equip you to fulfill it. He does not call the qualified. He qualifies the called.

If you want to live in the fullness of who God created you to be, there are some important steps you must take. First, surrender daily. Give God the space to shape and refine you into who He intended, rather than trying to force yourself into a version of success that was never meant for you. Second, surround yourself with people who encourage you in your faith, not those who make you feel like you need to be someone else to be accepted. Third, speak God's truth over your life. The world will try to tell you that you are not enough, but Scripture reminds you that you are chosen, loved, and called according to His purpose.

Lastly, take the next step. Maybe you do not know exactly what God is leading you to, but you do not need to have the whole plan to take the next step of obedience.

I want to challenge you to trust that God's design for you is good. No one else can fulfill the purpose He has placed on your life. The world does not need another imitation. It needs you to be who God created you to be. There is a deep peace that comes when you stop striving to be someone else and simply embrace the person God made you to be. It will take courage. It will require faith. But it will lead you into a life of purpose, joy, and freedom like nothing else can.

God is calling you to step into the fullness of who He created you to be. Do not let fear hold you back. Trust Him, walk in faith, and become the person He designed you to be.

The world is waiting for the real you.

HEART CHECK

- ✝ Am I trying to fit into a mold instead of embracing who God created me to be?
- ✝ Do fear and insecurity keep me from stepping fully into my calling?
- ✝ Am I seeking the approval of others more than the approval of God?
- ✝ Have I allowed comparison to steal my joy and confidence?
- ✝ Do I trust that God has designed me on purpose for a purpose?
- ✝ What step of obedience is God asking me to take today?
- ✝ Am I surrounding myself with people who encourage my faith and calling?
- ✝ Do I speak God's truth over my life, or do I allow doubt to shape my perspective?

Pray and Believe: *"Lord, I come before You with a heart that longs to fully embrace who You created me to be. I surrender my fears, insecurities, and the pressure to be someone I am not. Help me to trust that Your design for my life is intentional and good. Please give me the courage to walk boldly in my calling without fear of what others may think. Let me find confidence in Your approval alone, knowing that I am chosen, loved, and equipped for the purpose You have set before me. When I am tempted to compare myself to others, remind me that my worth is found in You alone. I ask for faith to take the next step, even when I do not have all the answers. Strengthen me to live as the person You created me to be, bringing glory to Your name. In Jesus' name, Amen."*

Take a moment to reflect on what God may be speaking to your heart. What is one step you can take today to embrace your identity in Him? Write it down, pray over it, and move forward in faith. God is calling you to be fully and confidently you.

CHAPTER 15

IT'S TIME FOR YOUR COMEBACK

It's time for your comeback. Not just someday, not when everything is perfect, not when you feel strong enough, but right now. Whatever has held you back, whatever has knocked you down, whatever has kept you from stepping fully into the life God has for you, it does not have the final say. God does. And He is calling you forward.

Life has a way of making us believe that we are stuck where we are. Maybe you have been through a season of loss or failure. Maybe your faith has been shaken, and you wonder if you will ever feel close to God again. Maybe you have let fear or discouragement keep you from moving forward. It does not matter how long you have been in this place. What matters is that you do not have to stay here.

God is not finished with you. He is not waiting for you to prove yourself or earn your way back. He is simply inviting you to take the next step. A comeback is not about pretending the past never happened. It is about letting God redeem it. He does not waste anything, not even the struggles, mistakes, or heartbreaks.

Everything you have walked through can be used for something greater when you put it in His hands.

Maybe you feel like you have been on the sidelines watching everyone else move forward while you stay stuck. But God never intended for you to sit in defeat. The enemy would love for you to believe that it is too late, that you have made too many mistakes, or that you are too far behind. That is not the truth. The truth is that God is a God of restoration. He is a God of second chances, new beginnings, and fresh starts.

A comeback starts with a decision. It does not happen overnight, and it does not require you to have everything figured out. It just requires you to say yes to God again. Maybe that means renewing your commitment to Him, stepping back into the calling you walked away from, or simply believing again that He has a purpose for you. Whatever it is, the time is now.

Fear will try to stop you. It will tell you to wait until you feel more ready. It will remind you of all the reasons you think you cannot do this. But God has never asked you to do it alone. He is the one who strengthens, restores, and leads the way. All He needs from you is a willing heart.

You may not see it yet, but something is shifting. God is moving on your behalf. What felt impossible yesterday is already being made possible in His timing. What felt broken is being restored. What felt lost is being redeemed. The comeback is not just something you wish for. It is something God has already prepared for you.

This is not the end of your story. In fact, it is just the beginning of something new. No more sitting in the past. No more believing the lie that you are not worthy of a fresh start. No more waiting for the perfect conditions. It is time. It is time to step forward. It is time to believe again. It is time to trust that God's plan for you is still good.

You are not alone in this. God is with you, and He always has been. Even in the moments when you felt forgotten, even in the seasons where you thought you had nothing left, He was there. He has been preparing you for this moment, for this next step, for this comeback that will be bigger than you imagined.

The return of the believer is not just about looking back at where you have been. It is about stepping fully into who God has called you to be. This is your moment. This is your time. It is time for your comeback.

HEART CHECK

- ✝ Do I believe that God still has a purpose for me, no matter where I have been or what I have been through?
- ✝ Have I allowed fear, shame, or discouragement to keep me from stepping into what God has for me?
- ✝ Am I waiting for the perfect conditions to move forward instead of trusting God's timing?
- ✝ Do I see my past as something that disqualifies me, or am I willing to let God redeem it for His glory?
- ✝ Have I been sitting on the sidelines when God is calling me to step forward in faith?
- ✝ Do I trust that God's strength is enough, even when I feel weak?
- ✝ What is one step I can take today to say yes to God's plan for my life?
- ✝ As I finish this book, what has God been speaking to my heart, and how will I respond?

Pray and Believe: *"Lord, I come before You ready for what is next. I let go of the past, the doubts, and the fear that have kept me from stepping forward. I receive Your strength, Your grace, and the comeback You have prepared for me. I trust that You are not finished with me and that my best days are still ahead. Lead me, guide me, and help me walk boldly into the purpose You have for my life. Thank You for never giving up on me. I am ready. In Jesus' name, Amen."*

Please take a moment to reflect. This is not just the end of a book. This is the beginning of something new. What has God spoken to you through these pages? What step is He calling you to take? Write it down, pray over it, and move forward with confidence. Your comeback starts now.

SECTION 2

KEY VERSES FOR PRAYER, STUDY, AND MEDITATION

This section provides a collection of powerful scriptures designed to deepen your faith, strengthen your prayer life, and guide your daily walk with God. These verses serve as a foundation for reflection of what you've read, offering wisdom, encouragement, and direction in various seasons of life. By meditating on these passages, you can grow spiritually, gain insight into God's promises, and develop a stronger connection with Him through prayer and study.

While all the verses in this section are presented in the New Living Translation (NLT) for clarity and readability, it is beneficial to study them in multiple translations to gain a more well-rounded understanding of Scripture.

Different translations can highlight various nuances in meaning, wording, and depth, helping to uncover the richness of God's Word. Comparing versions like the NIV, ESV, KJV, NKJV, CSB, or NASB can provide deeper insight into key themes, theological concepts, and the original intent of the text. This practice encourages a more holistic approach to Bible study, allowing for greater comprehension and personal application.

> ## MARK 11:20-25 (NLT)

The next morning as they passed by the fig tree he had cursed, the disciples noticed it had withered from the roots up. Peter remembered what Jesus had said to the tree on the previous day and exclaimed,

"Look, Rabbi! The fig tree you cursed has withered and died!"

Then Jesus said to the disciples,

"Have faith in God. I tell you the truth, you can say to this mountain, 'May you be lifted up and thrown into the sea,' and it will happen. But you must really believe it will happen and have no doubt in your heart. I tell you, you can pray for anything, and if you believe that you've received it, it will be yours. But when you are praying, first forgive anyone you are holding a grudge against, so that your Father in heaven will forgive your sins, too."

> **MALACHI 3:7 (NLT)**
>
> Ever since the days of your ancestors, you have scorned my decrees and failed to obey them. **Now return to me, and I will return to you,**" says the Lord of Heaven's Armies. "But you ask,
>
> *'How can we return when we have never gone away?'*

> **PSALM 139:1-3 (NLT)**
>
> O Lord, you have examined my heart and know everything about me. You know when I sit down or stand up. You know my thoughts even when I'm far away. You see me when I travel and when I rest at home. You know I do.

> **JEREMIAH 1:5 (NLT)** _____
>
> "I knew you before I formed you in your mother's womb. Before you were born I set you apart and appointed you as my prophet to the nations."

> **LUKE 12:7 (NLT)** _____
>
> And the very hairs on your head are all numbered. So don't be afraid; you are more valuable to God than a whole flock of sparrows.

LUKE 15:20 (NLT)

So he returned home to his father. And while he was still a long way off, his father saw him coming. Filled with love and compassion, he ran to his son, embraced him, and kissed him.

> **ROMANS 8:38-39 (NLT)**

And I am convinced that nothing can ever separate us from God's love.

Neither death nor life, neither angels nor demons, neither our fears for today nor our worries about tomorrow—not even the powers of hell can separate us from God's love.

No power in the sky above or in the earth below—indeed, nothing in all creation will ever be able to separate us from the love of God that is revealed in Christ Jesus our Lord.

> **JOHN 10:10 (NLT)**

The thief's purpose is to steal and kill and destroy. My purpose is to give them a rich and satisfying life.

EPHESIANS 6:10-18 (NLT)

A final word: Be strong in the Lord and in his mighty power. Put on all of God's armor so that you will be able to stand firm against all strategies of the devil. For we are not fighting against flesh-and-blood enemies, but against evil rulers and authorities of the unseen world, against mighty powers in this dark world, and against evil spirits in the heavenly places. Therefore, put on every piece of God's armor so you will be able to resist the enemy in the time of evil. Then after the battle you will still be standing firm. Stand your ground, putting on the belt of truth and the body armor of God's righteousness. For shoes, put on the peace that comes from the Good News so that you will be fully prepared. In addition to all of these, hold up the shield of faith to stop the fiery arrows of the devil. Put on salvation as your helmet, and take the sword of the Spirit, which is the word of God. Pray in the Spirit at all times and on every occasion. Stay alert and be persistent in your prayers for all believers everywhere.

> **PSALM 23:4 (NLT)**

Even when I walk through the darkest valley, I will not be afraid, for you are close beside me. Your rod and your staff protect and comfort me.

> **LUKE 15:22-24 (NLT)**

"But his father said to the servants,

'Quick! Bring the finest robe in the house and put it on him. Get a ring for his finger and sandals for his feet. And kill the calf we have been fattening. We must celebrate with a feast, for this son of mine was dead and has now returned to life. He was lost, but now he is found.'

> **REVELATION 3:16 (NLT)**
>
> But since you are like lukewarm water, neither hot nor cold, I will spit you out of my mouth!

> **MATTHEW 13:22 (NLT)**
>
> The seed that fell among the thorns represents those who hear God's word, but all too quickly the message is crowded out by the worries of this life and the lure of wealth, so no fruit is produced.

> **GALATIANS 6:7 (NLT)** _____

Don't be misled—you cannot mock the justice of God. You will always harvest what you plant.

> **ROMANS 3:23 (NLT)** _____

For everyone has sinned; we all fall short of God's glorious standard.

1 JOHN 1:9 (NLT)

But if we confess our sins to him, he is faithful and just to forgive us our sins and to cleanse us from all wickedness.

LUKE 8:25 (NLT)

Then he asked them,

"Where is your faith?"

The disciples were terrified and amazed.

"Who is this man?"

They asked each other.

"When he gives a command, even the wind and waves obey him!"

ACTS 4:12 (NLT)

There is salvation in no one else! God has given no other name under heaven by which we must be saved.

PROVERBS 16:15 (NLT)

When the king smiles, there is life; his favor refreshes like a spring rain.

JOSHUA 1:5-9 (NLT)

No one will be able to stand against you as long as you live. For I will be with you as I was with Moses. I will not fail you or abandon you. Be strong and courageous, for you are the one who will lead these people to possess all the land I swore to their ancestors I would give them. Be strong and very courageous. Be careful to obey all the instructions Moses gave you. Do not deviate from them, turning either to the right or to the left. Then you will be successful in everything you do. Study this Book of Instruction continually. Meditate on it day and night so you will be sure to obey everything written in it. Only then will you prosper and succeed in all you do. This is my command—be strong and courageous! Do not be afraid or discouraged. For the Lord your God is with you wherever you go.

> **1 JOHN 5:17 (NLT)**

All wicked actions are sin, but not every sin leads to death.

> **GALATIANS 5:19-21 (NLT)**

When you follow the desires of your sinful nature, the results are very clear: sexual immorality, impurity, lustful pleasures, idolatry, sorcery, hostility, quarreling, jealousy, outbursts of anger, selfish ambition, dissension, division, envy, drunkenness, wild parties, and other sins like these. Let me tell you again, as I have before, that anyone living that sort of life will not inherit the Kingdom of God.

> **ROMANS 1:29-32 (NLT)** _____
>
> Their lives became full of every kind of wickedness, sin, greed, hate, envy, murder, quarreling, deception, malicious behavior, and gossip. They are backstabbers, haters of God, insolent, proud, and boastful. They invent new ways of sinning, and they disobey their parents. They refuse to understand, break their promises, are heartless, and have no mercy. They know God's justice requires that those who do these things deserve to die, yet they do them anyway. Worse yet, they encourage others to do them, too.

> **ISAIAH 1:18 (NLT)**

"Come now, let's settle this," says the Lord. "Though your sins are like scarlet, I will make them as white as snow. Though they are red like crimson, I will make them as white as wool."

> **GALATIANS 5:22-23 (NLT)**

But the Holy Spirit produces this kind of fruit in our lives: love, joy, peace, patience, kindness, goodness, faithfulness, gentleness, and self-control. There is no law against these things!

> **LUKE 9:23 (NLT)** _____

Then he said to the crowd,

"If any of you wants to be my follower, you must turn from your selfish ways, take up your cross daily, and follow me."

> **GALATIANS 5:24 (NLT)** _____

Those who belong to Christ Jesus have nailed the passions and desires of their sinful nature to his cross and crucified them there.

> **1 CORINTHIANS 10:13 (NLT)**

The temptations in your life are no different from what others experience. And God is faithful. He will not allow the temptation to be more than you can stand. When you are tempted, he will show you a way out so that you can endure.

> **MATTHEW 16:25 (NLT)**

If you try to hang on to your life, you will lose it. But if you give up your life for my sake, you will save it.

>

JOHN 14:15 (NLT) _____

"If you love me, obey my commandments."

>

1 THESSALONIANS 5:14 (NLT) _____

Brothers and sisters, we urge you to warn those who are lazy. Encourage those who are timid. Take tender care of those who are weak. Be patient with everyone.

> **LUKE 5:16 (NLT)**

But Jesus often withdrew to the wilderness for prayer.

> **HEBREWS 4:12 (NLT)**

For the word of God is alive and powerful. It is sharper than the sharpest two-edged sword, cutting between soul and spirit, between joint and marrow. It exposes our innermost thoughts and desires.

>

MATTHEW 5:27-28 (NLT) _____

"You have heard the commandment that says, 'You must not commit adultery.' But I say, anyone who even looks at a woman with lust has already committed adultery with her in his heart."

>

PROVERBS 4:23 (NLT) _____

Guard your heart above all else, for it determines the course of your life.

> **PHILIPPIANS 4:8 (NLT)**
>
> And now, dear brothers and sisters, one final thing. Fix your thoughts on what is true, and honorable, and right, and pure, and lovely, and admirable. Think about things that are excellent and worthy of praise.

> **2 CORINTHIANS 10:5 (NLT)**
>
> We destroy every proud obstacle that keeps people from knowing God. We capture their rebellious thoughts and teach them to obey Christ.

> **PSALM 51:10 (NLT)** _____

Create in me a clean heart, O God. Renew a loyal spirit within me.

> **1 SAMUEL 16:7 (NLT)** _____

But the Lord said to Samuel,

"Don't judge by his appearance or height, for I have rejected him. The Lord doesn't see things the way you see them. People judge by outward appearance, but the Lord looks at the heart."

> **JAMES 2:1 (NLT)**

My dear brothers and sisters, how can you claim to have faith in our glorious Lord Jesus Christ if you favor some people over others?

> **PROVERBS 18:12 (NLT)**

Haughtiness goes before destruction; humility precedes honor.

> **MATTHEW 23:12 (NLT)**
>
> But those who exalt themselves will be humbled, and those who humble themselves will be exalted.

PHILIPPIANS 2:5-9 (NLT)

You must have the same attitude that Christ Jesus had. Though he was God, he did not think of equality with God as something to cling to. Instead, he gave up his divine privileges; he took the humble position of a slave and was born as a human being. When he appeared in human form, he humbled himself in obedience to God and died a criminal's death on a cross. Therefore, God elevated him to the place of highest honor and gave him the name above all other names, that at the name of Jesus every knee should bow, in heaven and on earth and under the earth, and every tongue declare that Jesus Christ is Lord, to the glory of God the Father.

> **PROVERBS 16:18 (NLT)** _____

Pride goes before destruction, and haughtiness before a fall.

> **DANIEL 4:30 (NLT)** _____

As he looked out across the city, he said, "Look at this great city of Babylon. By my own mighty power, I have built this beautiful city as my royal residence to display my majestic splendor."

> **JAMES 4:6 (NLT)**

And he gives grace generously. As the Scriptures say, "God opposes the proud but gives grace to the humble."

> **LUKE 14:11 (NLT)**

For those who exalt themselves will be humbled, and those who humble themselves will be exalted.

>

HABAKKUK 2:3 (NLT) _____

This vision is for a future time. It describes the end, and it will be fulfilled. If it seems slow in coming, wait patiently, for it will surely take place. It will not be delayed.

>

ROMANS 8:28 (NLT) _____

And we know that God causes everything to work together for the good of those who love God and are called according to his purpose for them.

> **PHILIPPIANS 1:6 (NLT)**

And I am certain that God, who began the good work within you, will continue his work until it is finally finished on the day when Christ Jesus returns.

> **PSALM 37:23 (NLT)**

The Lord directs the steps of the godly. He delights in every detail of their lives.

> **2 TIMOTHY 1:7 (NLT)** _____

For God has not given us a spirit of fear and timidity, but of power, love, and self-discipline.

> **JAMES 4:8 (NLT)** _____

Come close to God, and God will come close to you. Wash your hands, you sinners; purify your hearts, for your loyalty is divided between God and the world.

> **LUKE 8:25 (NLT)**

Then he asked them,

"Where is your faith?"

The disciples were terrified and amazed.

"Who is this man?"

They asked each other.

"When he gives a command, even the winds and waves obey him!"

> **ACTS 3:19 (NLT)** _____

Now repent of your sins and turn to God, so that your sins may be wiped away.

> **MATTHEW 11:28 (NLT)** _____

Then Jesus said,

"Come to me, all of you who are weary and carry heavy burdens, and I will give you rest."

LUKE 15:18-20 (NLT)

I will go home to my father and say,

'Father, I have sinned against both heaven and you, and I am no longer worthy of being called your son. Please take me on as a hired servant.'

So he returned home to his father, and while he was still a long way off, his father saw him coming. Filled with love and compassion, he ran to his son, embraced him, and kissed him.

>

2 TIMOTHY 1:7 (NLT) _____

For God has not given us a spirit of fear and timidity, but of power, love, and self-discipline.

>

PSALM 139:13-14 (NLT) _____

You made all the delicate, inner parts of my body and knit me together in my mother's womb. Thank you for making me so wonderfully complex! Your workmanship is marvelous—how well I know it.

❝

GALATIANS 1:10 (NLT)

Obviously, I'm not trying to win the approval of people, but of God. If pleasing people were my goal, I would not be Christ's servant.

Made in the USA
Columbia, SC
01 April 2025